This book belongs to

_ _ _ _ _ _ _ _ _ _ _ _ _ _

Ninja Life Hacks®
by Mary Nhin

Nervous Ninja

A Social Emotional Learning Book About Calming Worry and Anxiety

Ninja Life Hacks
by Mary Nhin

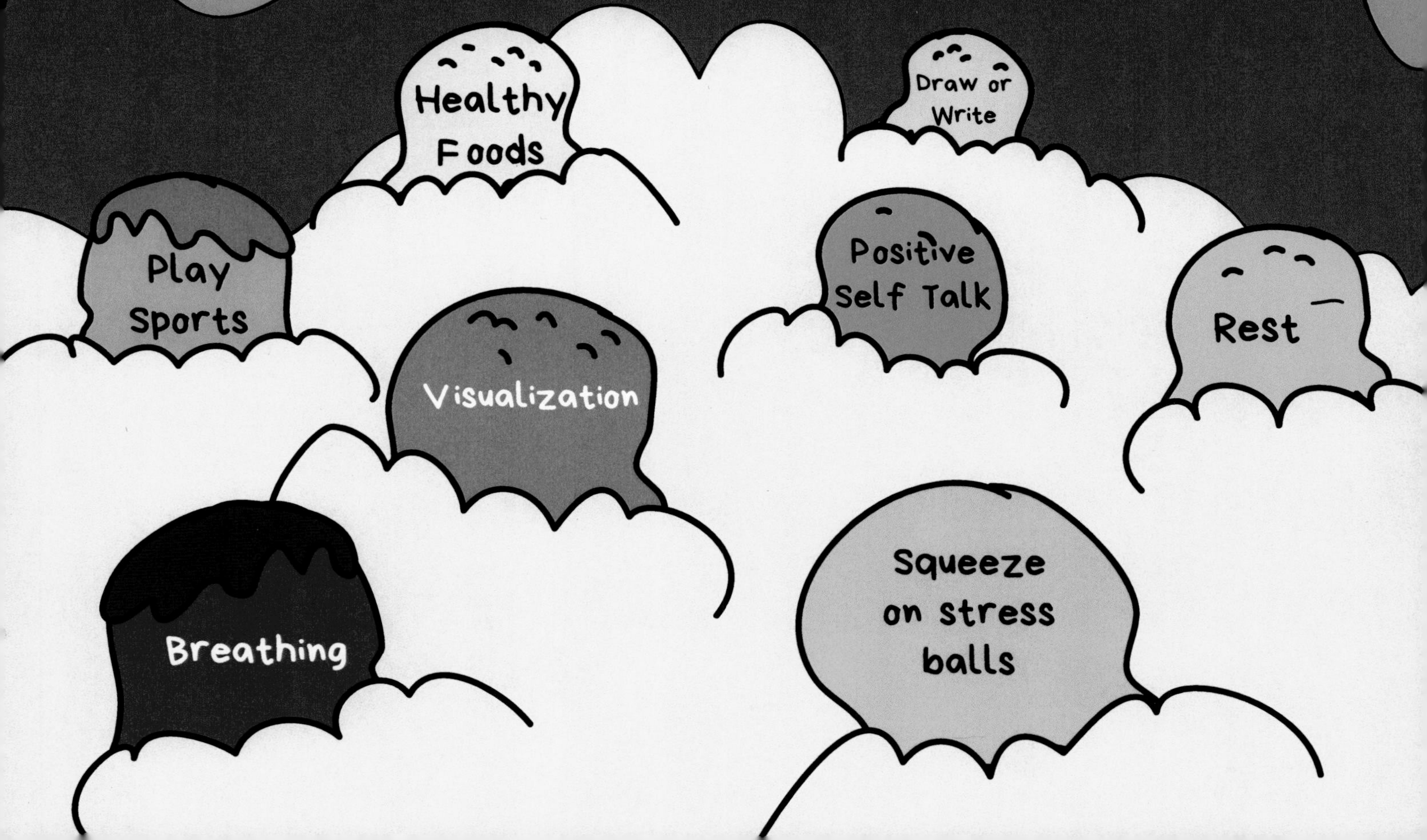

Healthy Foods

Draw or Write

Play Sports

Positive Self Talk

Rest

Visualization

Breathing

Squeeze on stress balls

Hi, I'm Nervous Ninja. Today, I'm going to share a story with you about a ninja life hack called calming cones. It helps me when I'm feeling nervous. I hope it helps you, too.

It was recess on the first day back at school and I was nervous. Everything was all right so far, but this just made me think that something would go wrong soon!

The day before, I couldn't find my shoes. I
looked everywhere and got very upset.

My mom heard the fuss and came to ask what the matter was. When I said I couldn't find my shoes, she was very apologetic. She had taken the shoes to get a new pair! My mom knew I liked that style, but my feet had grown!

Then, I began to worry about my new teacher and my classmates. Who would they be? Would they like me? What new rules would there be at school?

I worried about it all through dinner, while I showered, and when I was in bed, trying to fall asleep!

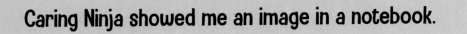
Caring Ninja showed me an image in a notebook.

CALMING CONES

Visualization

Breathing

Healthy Foods

Positive Self Talk

Rest

Go Outside

Exercise

Draw or Write

Play Sports

Talk about it

Spend time with animals

Yoga

Squeeze on stress balls

Listen to music

Caring Ninja took in a deep breath and held it for a second or two, then released it slowly. "Like that! Together now!" We breathed together several times.

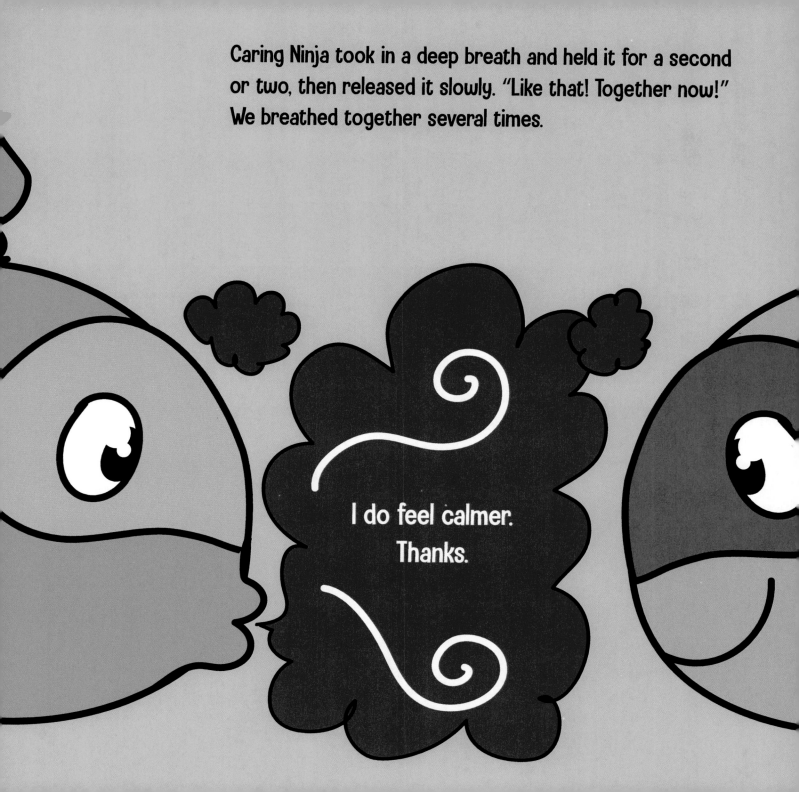

I do feel calmer. Thanks.

I opened my mouth to say, 'I can't,' again but said "I can!" instead.

The next day we were at gym class. I had gone to bed early and had a good night's sleep. I was refreshed and ready to do my best. Coach really was big and scary. I took five deep breaths and said a timid...

Coach gave me a tiny nod that made me feel a little bit braver.

"I can do sports and will make myself proud!" I said to myself.

It seemed Coach had really good ears. "I'm pleased to hear it," he said, smiling at me.

Remembering to build yourself a calming ice cream cone could be your secret weapon in being less nervous!

Check out the Nervous Ninja lesson plans that contain fun activities to support the social, emotional lesson in this story at ninjalifehacks.tv!

I love to hear from my readers.
Write to me at info@ninjalifehacks.tv or send me mail at:

Mary Nhin
6608 N Western Avenue #1166
Oklahoma City, OK 73116

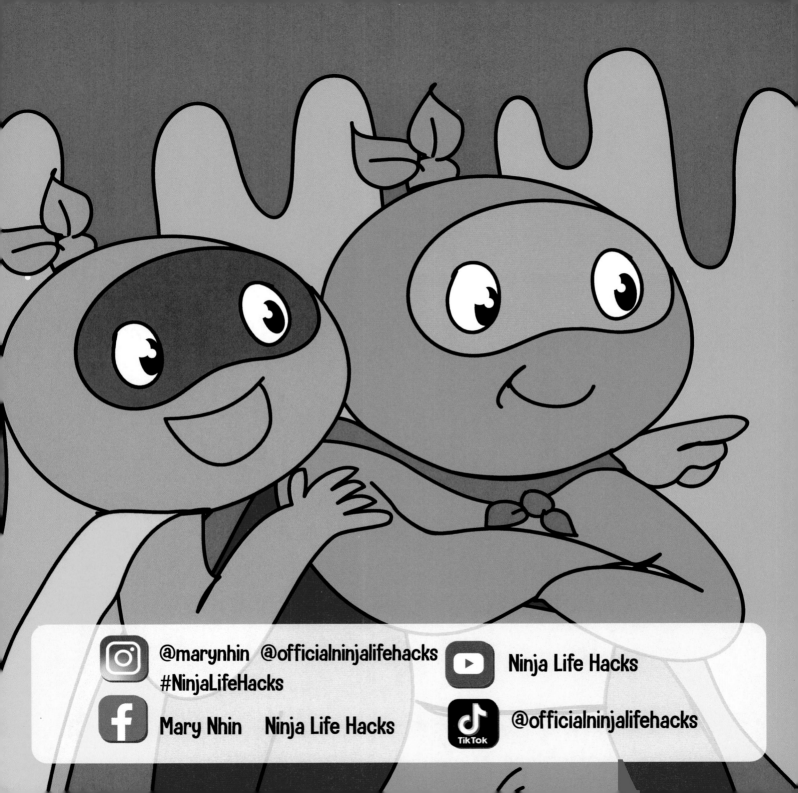

Made in the USA
Coppell, TX
03 October 2024

38029764R00024

TRIO GRANDE
ADIOS PALOMITA

writers
Olivier VATINE
Alain CLÉMENT

★

illustrators
Fabrice LAMY
Olivier VATINE

★

colorist
Isabel RABAROT

★

translated by **Mary Irwin**
edited by **Greg S. Baisden**
lettered by **Roxanne Starr**
with **Shannon Stewart**

Thanks to
Lib Héliot,
and Christophe & Philippe Lorin

TRIO GRANDE IN "ADIOS PALOMITA"

Written by Olivier Vatine & Alain Clément • Illustrated by Fabrice Lamy • Colors by Isabelle Rabarot • Translated by Mary Irwin • Scripted by Greg S. Baisden • Lettered by Roxanne Starr

¿NO PASÓ NADA?

SO... THIS YOUR LITTLE PARADISE...?

AND HERE I THOUGHT EVE WAS A BLONDE!

OH, NOOO! NOT MARY!

YOU KNOW HER-- ESA RUBIA?

ENOUGH SPLASHING AROUND! GET OUT-- WITH YOUR HANDS IN THE AIR!

ALL THE SAME, JOE--A BRUNETTE?

I REMEMBER A TIME WHEN THERE WAS SOMETHING YOU COULDN'T STAND ABOUT BRUNETTES...

YEAH--I REMEMBER...

THE SMELL!

¡JODIDA!

3

ALL THE SAME--IT'S INCREDIBLE!

5 YEARS SINCE WE LAST SET EYES ON EACH OTHER, AND WE'VE NO-THING TO SAY...!

...AT LEAST, YOU DON'T.

SO Y'MUST KNOW THET DOLORES WON'T HANG THERE FER LONG.

BE HONEST, MARY--Y'DIDN'T FIND ME B'ACCIDENT...

NO? DON'T TELL ME Y'DON'T KNOW 'BOUT HER BROTHERS?!

...MARY?

MM?

NOW THAT THINGS'RE QUIET... C'N I AST Y'ONE QUESTION?

FIRE AWAY...

WHUT EXACTLY Y'WANT, MARY?

FIRST, A DIVORCE!

?!!

SECOND, THE BOUNTY THAT'S BEEN ON YOUR HEAD FOR FIVE YEARS.

HUH?

FINALLY, MY SHARE OF OUR SAVINGS YOU HAVE STASHED AWAY --HERE IN MEXICO, I SUPPOSE...

HIC!

DOWN THERE. JOSEPH AND I CAME HERE SOMETIMES.

WE WOULD BATHE IN THE WARM SPRINGS, AND--

WELL... THERE'S A PAS- SAGE ABOVE, A SORT OF NATURAL CHIMNEY.

¡MUY BIEN! PACO AND FELIPE, TAKE THE ROPES AND GO DOWN THAT WAY!

JUAN AND I WILL COVER THE FRONT DOOR...

¡ENTENDIDO!

HOC!

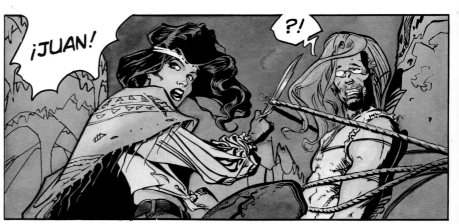

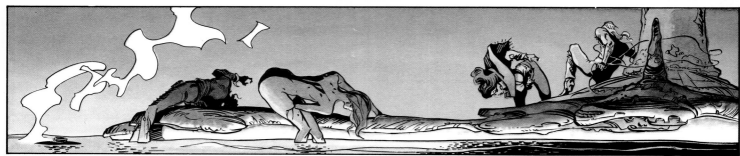

LOOK, HERE, DUMMY!

BRING OUT THET PILE O' WAN'ED NOTICES 'AT STILL GOT BOUNTIES OUT ON 'EM.

RIGHT AWAY, SHERIFF!

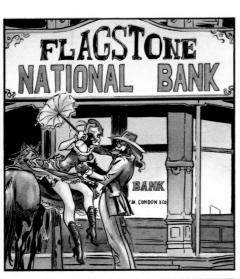

WHY?

...AHEM...

S'POSE Y'TELL ME FIRST HOW Y'WERE S' *DUMB* AS T'GIT CAUGHT B'THAT TIGHT-ASS SHERIFF?

WHAT!?!

YOU BASTARD! DON'T YOU DARE PULL THAT ON ME!

FIRST, *YOUR* FUCKING DYNAMITE PRACTICALLY KILLED MY HORSE! ALL THEY HAD TO DO WAS BEND DOWN AND PICK ME UP!

BELIEVE ME, JOSEPH, IT WAS YOUR LUCKY DAY! BY THE TIME THEY'D PATCHED THE SHERIFF TOGETHER, IT WAS DARK...

SO THEY WAIT TILL DAWN BEFORE GOING AFTER YOU.

BUT *ME*--THEY JAILED ME.

JUST LEFT ME THERE-- *TWO FULL DAYS,* AND ALL I DID WAS *PRAY* THEY WOULDN'T CATCH YOU...

AND LIKE A SILLY LITTLE FOOL, WHEN I SAW THEM COMING BACK EMPTY-HANDED...

I WAS OVERJOYED!

THAT'S... THAT'S PROBABLY HOW I COULD 'HANG ON' LIKE YOU SAID WHEN...

WHEN THE SHERIFF CAME TO QUESTION ME."

THERE... NOW, DO YOU NEED PRECISE DETAILS, OR HAVE I FINALLY *EARNED MY* ANSWER?

I'M DYING TO KNOW HOW THAT MEXICAN WOMAN MANAGED TO MAKE YOU FORGET YOUR WIFE WAS ROTTING AWAY IN JAIL!

WELL...

AL'RIGHT, S'MY TURN. B'T...YER GONNA BE DISAPPOINTED 'BOUT DOLORES...

Y'KNOW, WHEN I SAW YA IN TERCO'S ARMS, I DI'N'T HESITATE FER LONG--THERE *HAD* T'BE ANOTHER WAY THAN JUS' GIVIN' M'SELF UP!

I JUS' NEEDED T'FIND OUT *WHUT* THET WUZ...

"TH' FIRST TIME I WUZ ON TH' RUN *WITHOUT YA*...FELT VERY STRANGE. BUT I WEREN'T WORRIED FER YA, AN' I DI'N'T HAVE NO REGRETS, NO...BUT, DAMN, MARY! I WUZ *FURIOUS* WITH YA!! ALL THET *GOLD*, ENOUGH TO BLOW OFF A *HUNNERED YEARS* T'GETHER! AN' Y'LEFT ME ALL ALONE!"

"I HAD BUT ONE IDEA IN MIND-- *GET MARY!* STASH TH' GOODS 'N' GO GIT THET *STUPID* MARY!"

STASH THE GOODS 'N' GO...

?!!

B'T TH' MONTHS PASSED
AN' THEY FOUND NOTHIN...
ONE EVENIN', FEELIN'
DOWN, JASPER SOLD
HIS SHARE T'KOENIG...

BY A STROKE O' BAD LUCK,
TH' VERY NEXT DAY, 'BOUT
NOON, KOENIG STRUCK A
ENORMOUS VEIN O' GOLD!

NO NEED T'TELL YA, JASPER
FOUGHT DEARLY FER HIS
SHARE, B'T TH' OTHER GUY
KEPT EVERYTHIN' FER
HISSELF!
HEARTBROKEN, JASPER
WENT FAR AWAY AS
POSSIBLE. HE'D STOPPED
THERE, WHERE I FOUND
HIM, AND BEGAN T'DIG
AGAIN.

MEANWHILE, KOENIG'D
PROSPERED 'N' EXPANDED
--EVEN HAD A MINE NOT 15
MILES FROM JASPER'S
CLAIM!"

IF'N I FOLLA Y'RIGHT, YER LOOKIN' FER A SAFE SPOT T'STOW YER NEST EGG, WHILE Y'GO FETCH YER LADY-LOVE...?

WELL, NOW! THINK I GOT A' IDEA!

WHY NOT PUT YER GOLD *BACK* IN TH' BANK!?!

WHA-?

HAR HAR HAR! HIC! HIC!

HIC! HA HA HA!

JOE--NO! YOU DIDN'T!? YOU'RE NOT FOOL ENOUGH TO GO BACK TO A TOWN WITH YOUR PICTURE HANGING EVERYWHERE! NOT TO MENTION THAT THE OLD TIMER COULD SWIPE THE GOLD--*OUR* GOLD!--BEHIND YOUR BACK!

IF YOU'D'VE MET JASPER, YOU'D KNOW HE WEREN'T LIKE THET...

HIS IDEA WUZ PURE GENIUS--T'WUZ. FIRST OF ALL, 'CEPT WHEN YOU AN' ME'RE AROUND, *A BANK'S* TH' *IDEAL* PLACE T'HIDE YER BOOTY! AN' TH' OL' COOT PLANNED T'SETTLE HIS ACCOUNT WITH KOENIG AT TH' SAME TIME!

I DON'T GET IT...

I WUZ THE ONE GONNA MAKE TH' DEPOSIT, ALL TH' WHILE LETTIN' IT BE KNOWN *LOUD 'N' CLEAR* THET I WUZ TH' *NEPHEW* O' JASPER N. LYNCHBURG, JUS' ARRIVED FROM TH' EAST, AN' THET M'UNCLE'D JUS' STRUCK *TH' VEIN O' TH' CENTURY!*

WHUT I WUZ DEPOSITIN' WUZ *JUS'* A "LI'L GIFT" FROM 'IM T'HELP M'START OUT IN LIFE!

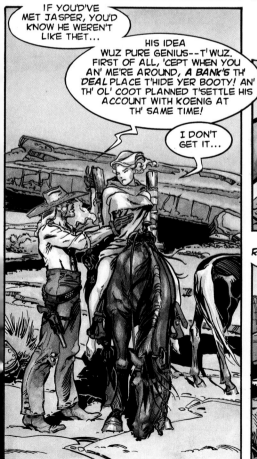

BUT THAT'S *RIDICULOUS!!* UTTERLY RI-DI-CUL-OUS!

NOT QUITE. WE CHOSE A BANK IN EL BRAVO, DOWN SOUTH NEAR THE BORDER. EVEN SO, WE TOOK PRE-CAUTIONS...

BOY, YER JUS' TH' NEPHEW I ALWAYS DREAMED ABOUT!

YEE-EP!

"Y'KNOW, MARY, YOU 'N' ME, WE BEEN ON SOME ROUGH TRAILS--B'T NEVER ON A *MULE!* RIDE LIKE THET I WOULDN'T WISH ON M'WORST ENEMY...

ONCE IN EL BRAVO, I STARTED T'SWEAT—I WUZ *SURE* SOMEUN'D RECOGNIZE ME ANY MINUTE! B'T I SOON SAW I HADD *NOTHIN'* T'WORRY 'BOUT ON THET SCORE..."

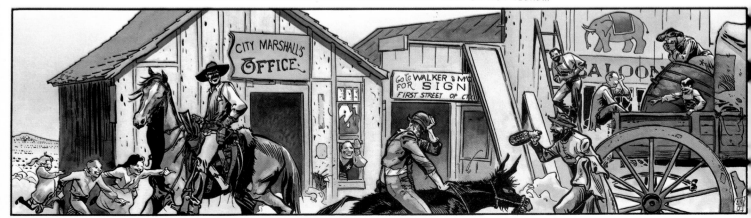

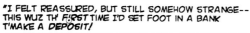
"I FELT REASSURED, BUT STILL SOMEHOW STRANGE-- THIS WUZ TH' *FIRST* TIME I'D SET FOOT IN A BANK T'MAKE A *DEPOSIT!*

JUS' TH' SAME, I DID MY LI'L NUMBER FER JASPER...

AN' IT WUZ FUNNY, TH' LOO[K] THEIR EYES--A LI'L JEALO[US] A LOT MAD AS HELL!

EVEN TH' GENT AT TH' COUNTER LOOKED SICK 'S HE WEIGHED TH' GOLD AN' TRIED T'KEEP HIS HANDS FROM TREMBLIN'....

YEAH, I GOT T'ADMIT--IN M'ROLE AS A SELF-SATISFIED MORON, I WUZ PURTY CONVINCIN'!

AN' SO, HE STAMP[ED] M'RECEIPT...

I HAD T'CLENCH M'TEETH SO AS NOT T'SHOUT FER JOY! I COULD BARELY WAIT T'GIT OUTSIDE!

B'T...I DI'N'T GIT TH' CHANCE...

¡¡MEDIA VUELTA, CRETINO!!

GULP!

'CUZ THA'S WHEN I MET DOLORES."

¡ARRIBA LAS MANOS, GRINGOS!

" ALL OF A SUDDEN, ONE O' TH' CUSTOMERS MUST'VE THOUGHT HE SAW PAT GARRETT...

IT WAS A *MASSACRE!*

THEY DI'N'T SHOOT ME ON TH' SPOT, THA'S ONLY 'CUZ THEY NEEDED A HOSTAGE T'COVER THEIR GETAWAY!

I WUZ SOON SORRY JASPER 'N' I HADN'T PICKED ANOTHER BANK, LIKE SOMEWHERE IN TH' BACKWOODS O' CANADA... IN NO TIME, WE WUZ AT TH' *RIO GRANDE!*...

THE BORDER...

THEY WERE HOME!

...AN' IT WUZ QUICKLY *CLEAR* THEY DI'N'T NEED ME NO MORE...!

ESPERATE UN MOMENTO.

LUCKY FER ME... EH... DOLORES SMILED.

I...NOTICED LATER THAT WHEN SHE SMILED THAT SMILE, TH' CRUELEST BASTARDS'D MELT..."

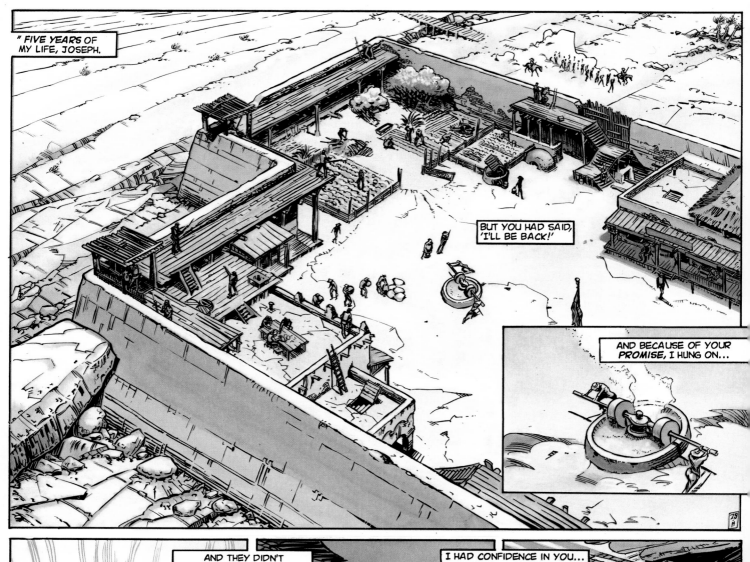

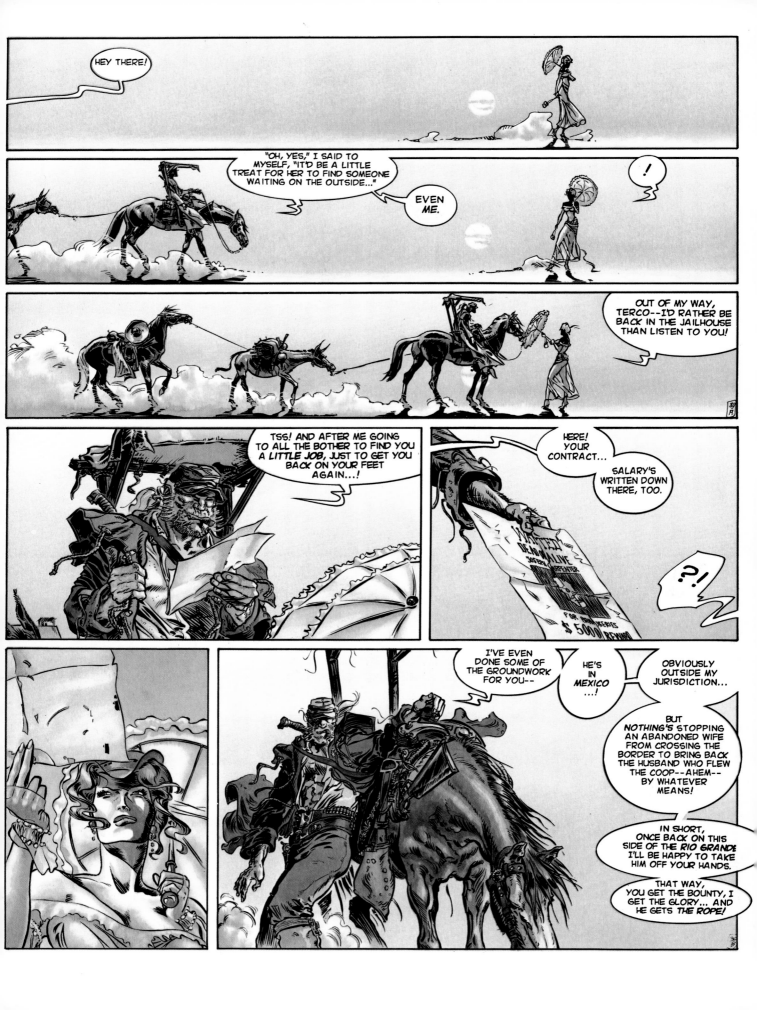

AND IN CASE YOU NEED ME, I WON'T BE VERY FAR BEHIND--AS A TOURIST, NOT WITH A CATAPULT!

OH! ONE MORE DETAIL: YOUR GOOD MAN, OVER THERE IN MEXICO--HE AIN'T EXACTLY LIVING *ALONE!* IF YOU GET MY DRIFT.

WHAT?!?

B'T...TH' *BORDER*-- THIS'S IT!

AN' YA--! *NOW'S* TH' TIME Y'TELL ME THIS?!

WITH TERCO QUIETLY WAITIN' FER ME OVER THERE BEHIND HIS *GATLIN' GUN!?*

...*MARY!?!* TELL ME *IT AIN'T TRUE!*

...OH, MY GOD...

NOW I UNNERSTAND HOW PACO AN' FELIPE FELL INTA TH' GROTTO...

IT WUZ *HIM!*

I CAIN'T BELIEVE IT! THAT Y'WANT *REVENGE* I C'N UNNERSTAND!

BUT THAT Y'D GO DO TERCO'S *DIRTY WORK!?!*

AN' NOW, Y'EXPECT M'T' FOLLOW Y'QUIETLY T'TH' OTHER SIDE, MARY? HUH?!

I'D RATHER DIE!

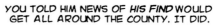

JOSEPH!

STRAIN YOUR BACK LAST NIGHT, OR DO YOU EXPECT ME TO SADDLE YOUR HORSE, TOO?

?!

YEP... THEM'S WOLF TRACKS ALL RIGHT!

HEH HEH!

JOSEPH...? COME ON, EVERYTHING'S READY!

YOU ARE REALLY A SLOW POKE!

JUS' A SEC, MARY. I'M COMIN'...

PROB'LY BEEN A WHILE SINCE HE DRUNK ANYTHIN' B'T WATER!

WHO? OH, YOU MEAN THAT--?

YEAH. I'M PURTY SURE BONANZA COME 'T' SEE US LAS' NIGHT...

WHUT SURPRISES ME'S THAT HE DI'N'T SHOW HISSELF...

B'T MEBBE HE'S GONE HALF WILD AG'IN SINCE JASPER DIED.

BAH!

DON'T WORRY! LIQUOR'S LIKE RIDING A HORSE--YOU DON'T FORGET IT!

NOW TELL ME HOW WE'LL GET THE GOLD BACK! AND WHICH ONE OF US GETS TO SAY, "THIS IS A HOLD-UP"?

NO, MARY, NO GUNS! I'VE HAD TH' RECEIPT IN M'POCKET FER FIVE YEARS, AN' I INTEND T'USE IT, O.K.?

PFF!

El Bravo

AND LET'S STOP ARGUIN'! IN 15 MINUTES, WE'LL BE LEADIN' NEW LIVES!!

AAA-MEN!

UH... HELLO!

Y'DON'T REMEMBER ME...?

!

FIVE YEARS AGO! TH' HOLD-UP? TH' FOUR MEXICANS, TOOK OFF WITH A HOSTAGE...?

THAT WAS ME!

OF COURSE! SO!! YOU... SURVIVED?!

NEVER FOUND A TRACE OF THEM! WELL! IF ANYONE HAD TOLD ME I'D BE SEEING YOU AGAIN!

ME, TOO! SAY--Y' REMEMBER THET SAME DAY, I WUZ IN HERE DEPOSITIN' SOME GOLD!

WE KNOW!

WELL, I'D LIKE T'WITHDRAW IT TODAY! EVEN KEP' M'RECEIPT!

EVERYTHING'S IN ORDER! ONLY, I'M THE MANAGER NOW! HERE'S OUR CLERK--

AND YOU'LL RUN NO RISK OF A HOLD-UP WITH HIM! HE'S A FORMER SHERIFF! HA HA!

OH?

?!

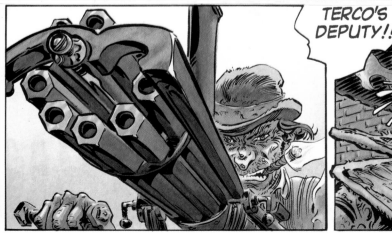

TERCO'S DEPUTY!!

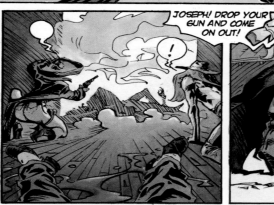

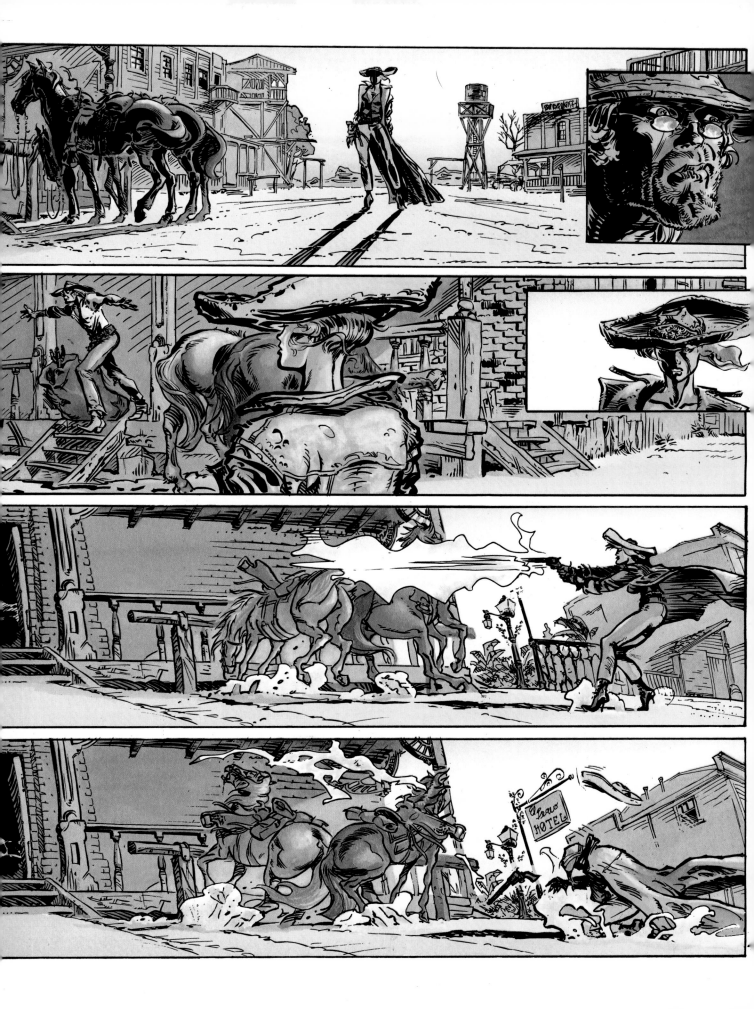

THE END

BOOKS TO READ

The very best in graphic literature—humor, horror, adventure and erotica!

Cherry's Jubilee

by Larry Welz & various artists
Adults Only. 40pgs, b&w,
$2.95

White Trash

by Gordon Rennie & Martin Emond
Mature Readers. 32pgs, full-color,
$3.95

Legends of Arzach

by R.J.M Lofficier, Moebius &
various artists Volumes 1-6,
full-color, $12.95

The Melting Pot Poster

by Simon Bisley
full-color, deluxe oversized,
$6.95

Madman

by Michael Dalton Allred
48pgs, 2 color
$3.95

Mr. Monster Atttacks!

by Michael T. Gilbert
& various artists
32pgs, full-color, $3.95

Taboo 7

edited by Stephen R. Bissette
Adults Only. 128pgs, b&w and
full-color, $14.95

Skin

by Peter Milligan, Brendan
McCarthy & Carol Swain
Adults Only. 48pgs, full-color,
$8.95

Wind of the Gods

by Cothias & Adamov
Mature Readers. 48pgs, full-color,
$14.95

Desperadoes

by Cromwell & Ruffner
Mature Readers. 48pgs, full-color,
$14.95

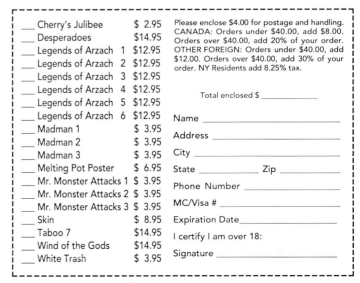

EXTRATERRESTRIAL DOGFIGHT

GROWING ZOMBIE HORDES

PAINTINGS BY CHARLES LANG
STORY BY KEVIN EASTMAN AND TOM SKULAN

SEND ME_____REGULAR 45 CARD BOXED
SETS AT $14.95 EACH
SEND ME_____DELUXE, SIGNED 51 CARD
LIMITED SETS AT $24.95 EACH
*PLEASE ENCLOSE $4.00 FOR POSTAGE AND HANDLING.
CANADA: ORDERS UNDER $40.00 ADD $8.00. ORDERS
OVER $40.00 ADD 20% OF YOUR ORDER. OTHER
FOREIGN: ORDERS UNDER $40.00, ADD $12.00, ORDERS
OVER $40.00, ADD 30% OF YOUR ORDER, NY RESIDENTS
ADD 8.25% SALES TAX.*

TOTAL ENCLOSED_____

NAME_____

ADDRESS_____

CITY_____STATE_____

ZIP_____PHONE #_____

MC/VISA #_____

EXPIRATION DATE_____

SIGNATURE_____

SEND TO: HEAVY METAL, DEPT. 0193
584 BROADWAY, SUITE 608
NEW YORK.NY 10012

ZOMBIE WAR TRADING CARDS!
ROARING ACTION FULL COLOR TRADING CARDS!!!
A ONE TIME ONLY X-MAS RELEASE
©1992 KEVIN B. EASTMAN AND TOM SKULAN.

TRIO GRANDE
ADIOS PALOMITA

written by Olivier Vatine & Alain Clément
illustrated by Fabrice Lamy & Olivier Vatine
translated by Mary Irwin
scripted & edited by Greg S. Baisden
lettered by Roxanne Starr
with Shannon Stewart

originally published in 1991 by Guy Delcourt Productions, Grenoble

North American Edition
Copyright © 1993 Tundra Publishing Ltd.
320 Riverside Dr., Northampton MA 01060
All Rights Reserved.

ISBN 1-879450-43-7